DISCARD

AFRICA

A LOOK BACK

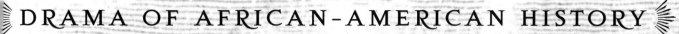

DRAMA OF AFRICAN-AMERICAN HISTORY

AFRICA
A LOOK BACK

by JAMES HASKINS and
KATHLEEN BENSON

mc **Marshall Cavendish**
Benchmark
New York

IN MEMORY OF LOUISE HASKINS

❀❀

ACKNOWLEDGMENTS

With thanks to Jill Watts, professor of history at California State University, San Marcos, for her helpful comments on the manuscript, and to the late Richard Newman, civil rights advocate, author, and senior research officer at the W. E. B. Du Bois Institute at Harvard University, for his thoughtful work in formulating the series.

The authors are grateful also to Jennifer N. Richardson for her assistance on the overall Drama of African-American History project. And special appreciation is due to the University of North Carolina at Chapel Hill Libraries for the invaluable online resource *Documenting the American South: North American Slave Narratives, Beginnings to 1920* (http://docsouth.unc.edu/neh/neh.html). This collection includes all the existing autobiographical narratives of fugitive and former slaves published as broadsides, pamphlets, or books in English up to 1920.

EDITOR: JOYCE STANTON   EDITORIAL DIRECTOR: MICHELLE BISSON
ART DIRECTOR: ANAHID HAMPARIAN   SERIES DESIGNER: MICHAEL NELSON

MARSHALL CAVENDISH BENCHMARK 99 WHITE PLAINS ROAD TARRYTOWN, NEW YORK 10591-9001

LIBRARY OF CONGRESS CATALOGING-IN-PUBLICATION DATA: Haskins, James, 1941-2005 Africa : a look back / by James Haskins and Kathleen Benson. p. cm.— (Drama of African-American history) Summary: "Provides a history of the roots of African-American culture, going back to the period of the transatlantic slave trade and earlier. Much of the history is told through reminiscences of slaves or former slaves in their 'narratives'"–Provided by publisher. Includes bibliographical references and index. ISBN-13:978-0-7614-2148-1 (alk. paper) ISBN-10:0-7614-2148-3 (alk. paper) 1. Slavery–United States–Juvenile literature. 2. Slaves–United States–Biography–Juvenile literature. 3. Slaves–Africa–Biography–Juvenile literature. 4. Slave-trade–Africa–History–Juvenile literature. 5. African Americans–History–To 1863–Juvenile literature. I. Benson, Kathleen. II. Title. III. Series. E446.H36 2007 967–dc22 2005030477

Images provided by Rose Corbett Gordon, Art Editor, Mystic CT, from the following sources: Cover: H. Tom Hall/National Geographic Society Collection; back cover: Private Collection/Bridgeman Art Library; pages i, x, 8, 41, 48: Private Collection/Bridgeman Art Library; pages ii–iii: Bibliothèque de l'Arsenal, Paris/Bridgeman Art Library; pages vi, 55: Mary Evans Picture Library; page viii: Special Collections, Connecticut College Library, New London; page xii: Sandro Vannini/Corbis; pages 3, 32: Werner Forman/Art Resource, NY; page 5: British Library/HIP/Art Resource, NY; pages 7, 16: National Museum, Lagos, Nigeria/Held Collection/Bridgeman Art Library; page 10: Bettmann/Corbis; page 12: Royal Albert Memorial Museum, Exeter, Devon/Bridgeman Art Library; page 14: Ethnologisches Museum, Staatliche Museen, Berlin/Bildarchiv Preussischer Kulturbesitz/Art Resource, NY; page 18: Werner Forman/Corbis; pages 19, 43: Stapleton Collection/Corbis; page 20: British Museum/Bridgeman Art Library; page 21: Indianapolis Museum of Art/Bridgeman Art Library; page 23: Corbis; page 24: The New York Public Library/Art Resource, NY; page 26: From Thomas Bluett: *Some Memoirs of the Life of Job, the Son of Solomon the Highest Priest of Boonda in Africa.* Documenting the American South (http://docsouth.unc.edu), The University of North Carolina at Chapel Hill Libraries, Rare Book Collection/UNC; pages 28, 36: Rare Books and Special Collections, Library of Congress; pages 29,39: Réunion des Musées Nationaux/Art Resource, NY; page 47: The Art Archive/Musée des Arts Africains et Océaniens/Dagli Orti; page 50: First Church of Christ, Congregational, East Haddam CT; page 53: The Art Archive/Biblioteca Nazionale Marciana Venice/Dagli Orti; page 56: Christie's Images/Corbis; page 61: Bojan Brecelj/Corbis.

Printed in China
1 3 5 6 4 2

On the title page: Slaves being marched to the West African coast from the interior, where they were captured

CONTENTS

INTRODUCTION

Africa: A Look Back is the first book in a series called the Drama of African-American History. The series begins with Africa because that is where African Americans' story began. As a matter of fact, Africa is probably where everyone's story began. The earliest remains of the ancestors of human beings have been discovered in Africa, which is often said to be the "cradle of humanity." But in this book we will look at Africa as it was during the time when its people were being captured and taken away as slaves.

For a long time in human history, much of the continent of Africa was almost unexplored by either Africans or outsiders, and not very much about the land was known. That was certainly so during the time of slavery, and it remained true even considerably later. Chapter 1 of this book is a brief introduction to Africa, focusing on its historical background in times before the transatlantic slave trade. Then, chapters 2, 3, 4, and 5 will look at the continent in more detail, with four men from Africa as guides: Olaudah Equiano, Ayuba ben Suleiman Diallo, Mahommah Baquaqua, and Venture Smith. These men lived about 250 years ago. All of them were captured in Africa and were taken far away as slaves, but each eventually had an opportunity to tell his story and have it appear in print in the United States or England.

African slavers transport their captives in a canoe.

The accounts by Olaudah, Ayuba, Mahommah, and Venture Smith are part of a fascinating and important group of historical documents called "slave narratives," in which slaves or former slaves tell of their experiences. About 150 such narratives were published as pamphlets or books; some became best sellers in their day; and some, including those by our four guides, have found an audience ever since. Beginning around 1825, many of the narratives had a purpose: to further the cause of abolishing slavery. In order to help bring an end to slavery, the narrators described harsh and brutal aspects of their lives as slaves. And simply by telling their stories, they wanted to help the reader, who might be prejudiced or ignorant, see them as fellow humans.

The cover page of Venture Smith's narrative, published in Connecticut in 1798

The narrators might also recall their earlier lives in Africa, giving details about families, religion, and so on. Our four guides do just that, so together, their narratives give us a sense of life in Africa during the time of the Atlantic slave trade. Olaudah wrote and published his book himself, but the others told their accounts to editors—and occasionally the white American or British editor had trouble understanding African names and wrote down some very odd words. The four stories vary in quality and completeness of information, and not everything in them has necessarily been studied or proved to be true. For example, it seems that sometimes a narrator is idealizing life in Africa—looking back on it with fondness and longing. Still, these men's memories of Africa are probably more accurate than observations made at the time by Europeans or white Americans.

Were the authors of slave narratives unusual, compared with the millions of Africans who were captured in their homeland and brought to North America, the West Indies, and Europe? In some ways, yes, they were unusual. First, as we have seen, they had a rare chance to present their stories to readers. Also, some of the narrators were educated in Africa. Of our four narrators, two were Muslims, and one of these was a Muslim cleric. That too is fairly unusual—Muslims may have made up only about one-tenth of the total number of slaves brought to the New World. Some slave authors had been born of royal blood. Some had managed to secure their freedom by purchasing themselves. One was actually able to return to his homeland. Finally, slave narrators do not represent all parts of Africa, although most of them did come from the same regions as the vast majority of slaves brought to the New World—west and central Africa.

Why are our four guides all men? The answer is that, unfortunately, no narratives of life in Africa by African-American slave women have been discovered. For example, Phillis Wheatley (1753?–1784) of Boston was a famous slave poet, but she had been kidnapped from her homeland at age six, and she said that she had almost no memories of Africa. The only experience she could recall was that at sunrise her mother poured out water as a kind of offering. (Most people have more memo-

Arab traders who traveled in caravans like this one in the Sahara learned and recorded a great deal about Africa.

ries of their early years; but possibly the shock of being taken from her mother and undergoing the horrors of the "middle passage"—the voyage across the Atlantic—caused a loss of memory in Phillis Wheatley.) Another female African slave, called Belinda of Boston, had been kidnapped at age twelve, but the only memories of Belinda's recorded in print were of the kidnapping itself.

Are slave narratives our only source of information about Africa? No, there are other sources. Actually, although Africans of course knew about their own ethnic group, kingdom, and culture, very few traveled far enough away from their own homes to learn much about other African cultures. Most of the early historical information about Africa comes from Arabs, who traveled considerably and had a long-established system of writing. Arab traders first traveled south to Africa by overland caravans. Many of them then settled down, bringing with them not only their trade goods but their own culture and their religion, Islam. Another source of information is Europeans, who came to Africa later than the Arabs and were also interested in trade. Europeans eventually colonized Africa and wrote about it, though often less open-mindedly than the Arabs. Although Africa had a rich culture, with great empires and kingdoms dating back thousands of years, Europeans tended to think of it as a land of savages because Africans were not Christians, and even as a land of nonhumans, because so many Africans were enslaved—the transatlantic slave trade was then at its peak.

The transatlantic slave trade and its effects on Africa are the topic of chapter 6, our final chapter. Here again, we will turn to our four guides for insights. Since this book is about the world the slaves came from, it is told, as much as possible, from the viewpoint of these individual Africans.

A NOTE ON DATES

A variety of systems of dating have been used by different cultures throughout history. Many historians now prefer to use BCE (Before Common Era) and CE (Common Era) instead of BC (Before Christ) and AD (Anno Domini), out of respect for the diversity of the world's peoples.

This statue from southern Egypt shows a Nubian man. Ancient Egypt was ruled by Nubian kings from about 760 BCE to about 656 BCE.

Chapter 1

Africa: A Brief History

AFRICA IS A HUGE CONTINENT WITH MANY DIFFERENT environments, cultures, and economies. Human societies in Africa date back 7,000 to 12,000 years before our own time—so long ago that the vast Sahara Desert did not yet exist.

AFRICA IN ANCIENT AND MEDIEVAL TIMES

In Africa, as around the world, prosperous civilizations developed along the major rivers. Between the years 4000 and 3000 BCE, the Egyptian and Nubian cultures thrived along the Nile River in northeastern Africa. The Egyptians and the Nubians developed advanced methods of farming; traded gold, ebony, ivory, and cattle with each other; and buried their kings and other important people in elaborate tombs filled with items that the dead might need in the afterlife.

Southward along the Nile River, in the area of present-day Sudan, was the wealthy and powerful civilization of Cush. For about a century, beginning in 750 BCE, Cushite kings ruled Egypt. Later, the Cushite capital was moved still farther south, to Meroë. Much of the economy of this kingdom was based on mining, smelting, and forging iron. Meroë may have been influential in spreading its iron technology to other parts of Africa, and by 180 BCE the kingdom had developed a system of writing.

Another ancient city was Jenne-Jeno, which archaeologists discovered quite recently in what is now the west African republic of Mali. Jenne-Jeno was founded around 250 BCE by herders and farmers who came there from a region of north-central Africa that is today southern Mauritania. Their original fertile homeland had become drier and drier after about 1000 BCE and eventually became a desert: the Sahara. This change impelled farmers and herders to leave, searching for new water sources. One source they reached was the great interior flood-plain of the middle Niger River, with its rich soil. There, they established Jenne-Jeno.

Over the next thousand years, Jenne-Jeno grew into a city of 10,000 people. It was protected by a massive mud-brick wall about ten feet thick and at least thirteen feet high. By 800 CE, Jenne-Jeno had a foundry where iron was forged and copper and bronze were molded into ornaments. However, what made Jenne-Jeno most prosperous was not ironworking but trade. At first, the city traded with the people of the Timbuktu region upriver to the north (Tombouctou, also in present-day Mali). Later Jenne-Jeno traded with North Africa. In exchange for Saharan salt, cloth, and Mediterranean glass beads, Jenne-Jeno

WHAT IS ARCHAEOLOGY?

Archaeology is the profession of people like those who discovered the ancient city of Jenne-Jeno. Archaeologists find out about the history of past human cultures by examining physical remains, from structures such as houses, walls, tombs, and bridges to artworks such as masks and jewelry, to daily objects such as pots and pans. The popular image of archaeologists "digging things up" isn't far from the truth. Often, they do have to unearth objects, and in fact their on-site work is known as a "dig."

How do archaeologists know where to dig? Sometimes they are guided by historical accounts, scriptures, stories, traditions, and even myths—one purpose of archaeological study may be to see how accurate an ancient writing or legend is. Often, archaeologists find buried remains by looking for certain features of the land lying on top, which may be mounded up in an unusual way or may show traces of an old road.

Archaeologists found this 600-year-old clay statue in the area around Jenne.

And how do archaeologists learn the age of what they find? One method of dating, as this process is called, is to look at layers, or strata, of earth. What layer an object lies in may reveal how old it is. Radiocarbon dating is another method, usable on objects made of material that was once alive. Living things contain carbon 14, which starts to decay at death, and the rate of decay can establish dates. There may also be clues such as inscriptions on walls and coins, artistic styles, and tools known to have come into existence at a certain time.

An archaeological discovery, whether it is as large as an entire city or as small as a fragment of pottery, helps us to understand and value our past.

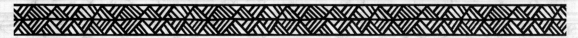

traded gold and copper jewelry and agricultural products such as red rice and onions. Jenne-Jeno remained an important trading city until the 1300s, but then, around 1400, it was abandoned and its people left for a new town nearby, called simply Jenne or Jenné.

One reason why Jenne-Jeno was abandoned may have been the increasing influence of North African Arabs. At that time, Arab traders had been in Africa south of the Sahara for hundreds of years, since about 500 BCE. They crossed the Sahara in carts drawn by horses or donkeys—later, they used camels—bringing spearheads, axes, glass, wine, and wheat to exchange for African gold, silver, copper, ivory, pepper, kola nuts, salt, and slaves. They may have established the new town of Jenne; but whoever established it, wealth and commerce became concentrated in Jenne, and more and more people of old Jenne-Jeno moved there.

Jenne in its turn became an important center of trade. By the 1600s, gold from mines far to the south was being transported overland to Jenne, then shipped on broad-bottomed canoes to Timbuktu. In Timbuktu, it was loaded onto camel caravans and transported across the Sahara to markets in North Africa and Europe. Jenne also shipped huge amounts of grain and dried fish to Timbuktu, which was surrounded by arid land and needed to get most of its food from elsewhere. Timbuktu was also an important city. In fact, from the 1300s to the 1600s it was one of the richest in Africa. It was a thriving center of trade and learning, with a famous university that drew Muslim scholars from near and far.

Still another important center of civilization was the kingdom, or empire, of the Songhai people. It began to expand in

A French traveler's depiction of the city of Timbuktu in the early nineteenth century

the fifteenth century under the ruler Sonni Ali. From the city of Gao, an important center on the middle Niger River south of Timbuktu, the Songhai conquered an ever-widening area. At the height of its power, in the late 1400s, the Songhai empire stretched from the Atlantic coast to what is now central Nigeria. It even conquered Jenne and Timbuktu. The influence of the Songhai empire ended, however, in the late 1500s, when its lands were invaded and conquered by Morocco.

There were other important and powerful trading empires on the west coast of Africa in these early times. One of them was Ghana, founded sometime around 400 CE. Ghana was a center of the iron industry, and it began to flourish along with the trans-Saharan trade. For eight hundred years—from about 450 to 1230—more gold was traded in Ghana than anywhere else in the world, and the Ghanian empire covered most of the territory between the Niger River and the Atlantic Ocean.

Another civilization was the Yoruba kingdom of Benin, in what is now southern Nigeria. Benin emerged in the 1200s and

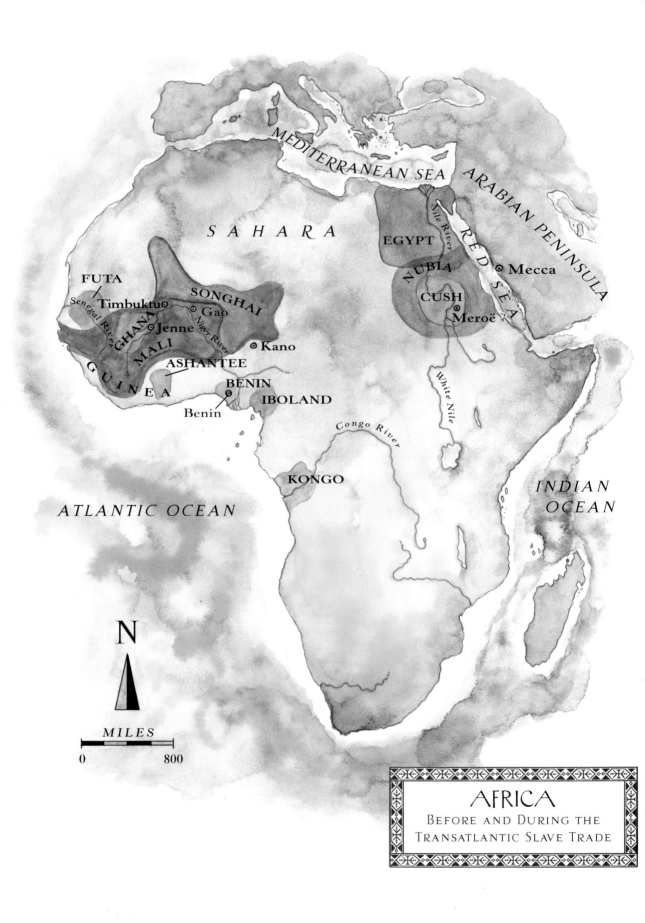

MEDITERRANEAN SEA

ARABIAN PENINSULA

SAHARA

EGYPT

NUBIA

Nile River

RED SEA

CUSH

Mecca

Meroë

FUTA

Senegal River

Timbuktu

SONGHAI

Gao

GHANA

Jenne

Niger River

MALI

Kano

ASHANTEE

GUINEA

BENIN

IBOLAND

Benin

Congo River

White Nile

KONGO

INDIAN
OCEAN

ATLANTIC OCEAN

N

MILES

0   800

AFRICA

BEFORE AND DURING THE
TRANSATLANTIC SLAVE TRADE

was at its most important in the 1400s. In its capital city, also called Benin, the red clay houses were polished to such a high luster that they looked like marble. Benin's craftspeople were very skilled. Their method of casting brass for sculpture was more advanced than that of Europe during the same time period.

The ancient city of Kano, also in present-day Nigeria, existed even before the Benin empire. Recent study of an impressive one-hundred-mile earthen wall near Kano indicates a time of about one thousand years ago. The wall, which was probably constructed over the course of three centuries, rises seventy feet from the bottom of a wide, deep ditch and surrounds several towns and villages, including the town of Eredo and Kano itself. All together, the wall encompasses about twenty-five miles from north to south and about twenty-two miles from west to east. According to local legend, it was ordered built by Bilikisu Sungbo, a wealthy, childless widow who wanted to leave a great monument in her own memory. Her grave lies near the wall in a town north of Eredo. If the legend is true, the wall certainly served her purpose: today, a thousand years later, it is known as Sungbo's Eredo.

Along with these large population centers in Africa, there were also small farm and village societies. These rural communities were, in certain ways, dependent on the great kingdoms. Although there was frequent warfare—which was the reason why large cities were enclosed by high walls and deep ditches—

This brass sculpture of a Portuguese soldier was made by one of Benin's skilled artists during the 1500s or 1600s.

the African kings did help to keep the peace in their own regions. Also, these kings encouraged the local economy. In addition to the small farms and villages, there were other, less populated rural areas. In Africa—as in many other places in the world, then and ever since—city dwellers and townspeople seem to have thought of the rural regions as being on the periphery, and of rural people as being backward. (Evidently, the stereotype of country bumpkins and city slickers goes back a long, long way.) Finally, there were great stretches of land, like the Sahara, which could not be used for agriculture. The few people who lived in these desert regions were nomadic—that is, they had no permanent settlements but continually moved from place to place. They traveled with camels and sheep, which provided their meat, and lived primarily on rice and dates, which they could carry with them.

Bedouins (*left*), nomads of the desert, approach a group of Egyptian peasants near the pyramids of Giza. This watercolor was painted by a German artist in 1859.

AFRICA AND THE EUROPEANS

During the 1400s the Portuguese began to explore the west coast of Africa. Soon they set up trading posts, and from these, colonies developed. It was the beginning of Europe's long period of influence in Africa. By 1700—the time when the drama of African Americans starts—the transatlantic slave trade would be under way. Before we turn to that era, it would be interesting to compare life on the two continents. Let's go back to the year 1500, about the time Europeans and Africans had their fateful encounter.

In 1500, Africa probably had a population of about 55 million, approximately the same as that of Europe. (However, Europe is much smaller in area than Africa.) In Africa, there were no national borders as we understand them today. Groups of people connected by blood ties or social obligations lived together, sometimes in towns and cities, more often in rural villages. In Europe, too, instead of well-organized, powerful nations like those of modern times, there were many kingdoms, city-states, and private territories ruled by nobles. The majority of Africans—as was also true of Europeans—were farmers. They spoke a great variety of languages and practiced different religions. Europeans also spoke several different languages. Most, though, practiced one religion: Christianity.

The prominent people in Africa usually combined both religious and political roles. These leaders, as noted earlier, helped to keep order and peace and encouraged the economy. In Europe, in most places, political and religious leaders played separate roles. Europeans and Africans differed in another important way: how they viewed their relationship to the land. In Africa, no one "owned" land. Instead, family and kinship

A busy marketplace in a village of central Africa. This illustration comes from a European expedition of around 1880.

groups held land in common. This was in sharp contrast to Europe, where land was owned by an elite class of monarchs, aristocrats, and church officials.

In Africa and in Europe, societies were organized as class systems. The lowest classes, at the bottom of the system, were the masses of people, who had few rights or privileges. In Europe, for example, people called serfs were peasants bound to the land, a social status that had been passed on from parents to children, generation after generation. Slavery was practiced in both Europe and Africa, and had existed on both continents for thousands of years. On both continents, too, people made war on one another for the same reasons: to consolidate power and to get by force what belonged to someone else.

By about the year 1700, the great kingdoms of Africa were in decline. The powerful Songhai empire, for example, had been conquered by the Moroccans in the north. The economies of the kingdoms suffered, too, as the once thriving trans-Saharan trade gave way to a new, seaborne trade between west Africa and Europe. Africa entered a difficult period of change and adjustment just when it was invaded by Europeans and struck by the transatlantic slave trade. Nothing on the continent would ever be the same again. Many west African economies became linked to the slave trade, with tragic results.

Most Europeans who went to Africa were intent on profit, or on bringing Christianity to people they considered savages. Few took the time to study the cultures from which the slaves came. Therefore, the most reliable sources of information on Africa in the time of the transatlantic slave trade include the people who wrote slave narratives—such as the four men who will be our guides in the following chapters.

After Olaudah Equiano was freed, he settled in England, where he married and became active in the movement to end the transatlantic slave trade.

Chapter 2

OLAUDAH EQUIANO

THE BEST-KNOWN AFRICAN SLAVE NARRATIVE is that of our first guide, Olaudah Equiano (1745?–1797), who was also called Gustavus Vassa—a name he had been given by one of his early owners. He published his autobiography himself in London in 1789. Its title is *The Interesting Narrative of the Life of Olaudah Equiano, or Gustavus Vassa, the African. Written by Himself.*

The Interesting Narrative contains a portrait of Olaudah. He was in his middle forties when his book was published, but we have the impression that he was one of those people who look about the same in middle age as when they were adolescents. He is shown as an oval-faced man with a high forehead, dressed as a British gentleman of the time, with a ruffled shirtfront and a high-collared coat with large buttons.

This brass plaque from Benin, made in about 1600, shows the traditional clothing of men in Olaudah Equiano's homeland.

The clothing that Olaudah wears in his portrait is very different from the attire of his African homeland. There, he wrote, "the dress of both sexes is nearly the same. It generally consists of a long piece of calico or muslin, wrapped loosely around the body, somewhat in the form of a highland plaid [Scottish traditional dress]. This is usually dyed blue, which is our favorite colour. It is extracted from a berry, and is brighter and richer than any I have seen in Europe. Besides this, our women of distinction wear golden ornaments, which they dispose with some profusion on their arms and legs." Golden ornaments must have been quite rare, because Olaudah tells us that his people had few luxuries. But they did have perfumes, which they made from a particular wood, beaten into powder and mixed with palm oil. Both men and women wore perfume.

Olaudah had been born around 1745, in Guinea, which was the name given by Europeans to a large area that extended some 3,500 miles along the west coast of Africa from the Senegal River to Angola. (Today it includes the nations of Guinea, Ivory Coast, Ghana, and Nigeria.) In Olaudah's time, this area had several kingdoms. It was the main region for the European slave trade.

Olaudah writes that his birthplace was Iboland (Ibo is one

of the main languages of present-day Nigeria). His kingdom was Benin, which he describes as the most important of the kingdoms in the region. It extended about 170 miles along the coast and nearly 1,500 miles into the interior and was divided into many provinces or districts. His own district was very far from the capital and the seacoast; in fact, he had never heard of white men, or of the sea. After he was kidnapped and enslaved at age eleven, he had several owners in Africa and traveled to different areas. He speaks of a town called Tinmah as the most beautiful place he had yet seen in Africa. He first tasted coconuts and sugarcane there.

Olaudah was born into a highly organized society. The king of Benin had absolute power. Below the king were lesser rulers—minor kings or chief men. Olaudah's father was a chief man. Olaudah says that his father had many slaves. The father also had many children, seven of whom lived to grow up. There was only one daughter. Olaudah was the youngest son and his mother's favorite. "She used to take particular pains to form my mind," he writes. "I was trained up from my earliest years in the art of war; my daily exercise was shooting and throwing javelins; and my mother adorned me with emblems after the manner of our greatest warriors."

If Olaudah had not been kidnapped and taken away, he would have been marked as a chief man. He describes the mark as a scar made "by cutting the skin across at the top of the forehead, and drawing it down to the eyebrows; and while it is in this situation applying a warm hand, and rubbing it until it shrinks up into a thick *weal* across the lower part of the forehead. Most of the judges and senators were thus marked; my father had long borne it: I had seen it conferred on one of my

A brass bust from Benin portraying the king's mother, the most powerful woman in the country. Her rank is shown by her crown of coral beads and the scars on her forehead, similar to those described by Olaudah Equiano.

brothers, and I was also destined to receive it by my parents."

Olaudah tells us that chief men such as his father came together in councils to settle disputes and punish crimes. Usually, the councils followed the "law of retaliation." Olaudah gives as an example a case that was heard by his father and the other judges. In this case, a man who was a chief or senator was charged with having kidnapped a boy, and even though he was an important person his punishment was to give up one of his own slaves.

The head of the family had the same kind of authority over his household as a king over a kingdom. A man could have more than one wife, but while a king might have many wives, the average man seldom had more than two.

As a rule, marriages were arranged by parents, although Olaudah knew men who had chosen their own wives. When a couple were betrothed, or promised to each other, a feast was held. The future bride and bridegroom stood up in the midst of all their friends and the man announced that the woman was to be looked on as his wife from then on. Then the bride was taken away, but the feast continued. Sometime later, the actual marriage took place, attended by the families of the young couple. The bride was delivered to the groom, with blessings. After that, she wore a cotton string tied around her waist, to signify that she was a married woman. Friends of the bride and bridegroom gave them land, slaves, cattle, household goods, and farm implements. In addition, the parents of the bridegroom presented gifts to the parents of the bride. Gifts were exchanged with great ceremony, and then everyone celebrated with bonfires, music, and dancing.

Olaudah's people were, he writes, "almost a nation of dancers, musicians, and poets. Thus every great event, such as a triumphant return from battle, or other cause of public rejoicing, is celebrated in public dances, which are accompanied with songs and music suited to the occasion. The assembly is separated into four divisions (married men, married women, unmarried men, unmarried women), which dance either apart or in succession, and each with a character peculiar to itself. . . . Each represents some interesting scene of real life, such as a great achievement, domestic employment, a pathetic story, or some rural sport; and as the subject is generally founded on some recent event, it is therefore ever new. This gives our dances a spirit and variety which I have scarcely seen elsewhere."

Olaudah says that his people had many musical instruments, including various drums and a stringed instrument that resembled a guitar (this is probably what came to be called a banjo in North America).

When children were born, people celebrated with dancing, feasts, and offerings. A child would be named for an event, characteristics, or circumstance. Olaudah's name, for instance, meant "fortune," "favor," and "being well-spoken."

In describing the religion of his people, Olaudah says that they believed in one "Creator of all things" who lived in the sun, wore a belt, and never ate or drank. Some people believed that the creator smoked a pipe, which was regarded as a great

MUSIC IN AFRICA

Olaudah tells us that his people were "almost a nation of dancers, musicians, and poets." That is completely true. In African cultures, music has been a very important part of life, with many functions, and with almost everyone participating in music making. Music is used for entertainment, for dancing, in plays, and in ceremonies. It also marks specific life events such as birth, coming of age, marriage, and death. Music often accompanies work, with special songs for, say, chopping wood, rowing a boat, or harvesting crops. There are even special songs when people are suing each other in a law court. And music is also a way of communicating: songs are used to pass on a group's history and to report and comment on current news. Songs and instrumental music are interwoven throughout the entire fabric of African life.

Olaudah's mention of poets is accurate, too, because there is a close link between music and language in Africa. In some African languages, the meaning of a word may depend on the pitch, tone, or musical note it is spoken in. And "talking drums" that can produce various pitches may be used to send messages.

Olaudah also says that his people had many musical instruments, and here too he is accurate. African instruments include bells, rattles, xylophones of many sizes, the mbira or "thumb piano," and of course numerous drums. Drums are so important that they have sometimes been considered as magical or holy—or as inhabited by the spirits of dead drummers—and have been kept in special sacred houses and even given offerings of food. And it has surely always been true that African drummers are among the best in the world.

Above: An Ibo musician pounds out a beat on two drums.

luxury among the Ibo. The people always spoke of God with great reverence. Consequently, Olaudah was shocked by the swearing he heard in Europe and America.

The sun and the moon were important to the Ibo. Olaudah writes, "We compute the year from the day on which the sun crosses the line; and, on its setting that evening, there is a general shout throughout the land; at least, I can speak from my own knowledge, throughout our vicinity. The people at the same time made a great noise with rattles not unlike the basket rattles used by children here [in England], though much larger, and hold up their hands to heaven for a blessing. It is then the greatest offerings are made."

The Ibo had no public places of worship. They practiced their religion wherever they happened to be. They were very clean people, according to Olaudah: "This necessary habit of decency was with us a part of religion, and therefore we had

Songs, music, and dance accompanied every great event celebrated in Olaudah's homeland, including these festivities in honor of the king.

many purifications and washings. . . . Those that touched the dead [for example] at any time were obliged to wash and purify themselves before they could enter a dwelling house."

Some Ibo believed, as Olaudah tells us, that when a person died, his or her soul took up residence in a newborn baby. Others believed that the spirits of the dead—especially relatives and close friends—remained with the living to protect them from the bad spirits of their enemies. For that reason, when those people sat down to eat, they would put a small portion of food and drink on the ground for the spirits. Also, they would often visit graves and would pour the blood of birds or other animals onto a grave as an offering. Olaudah remembers accompanying his mother to the grave of her mother, which he describes as a small thatched house set off by itself. He watched her pour blood on this grave and spent most of the night listening to her cries of grief.

People were buried with things that they might need in the afterlife. Olaudah recalls that when priests or wise men were buried, "most of their implements and things of value were interred along with them. Pipes and tobacco were also put into the grave with the corpse, which was always perfumed and ornamented, and animals were offered in sacrifice to them. None accompanied their funerals, but those of the same profession or tribe. These buried them after sunset, and always returned from the grave by a different way from that which they went."

Olaudah also tells us that the priests or wise men were heal-

This brass statue of a rooster may once have sat on a noble Ibo family's altar.

ers, and that they were very successful at healing wounds and at treating cases of poisoning. They could also identify criminals. Olaudah does not know how they did this, but he remembers one occasion when a young woman had been poisoned by an unknown enemy. The wise man ordered several other men to lift up the corpse and carry it to the grave by a particular route. As the men headed for the grave site, the body suddenly fell from their shoulders near a house. This was considered a clear sign that the owner of the house was the poisoner, and indeed he immediately confessed.

Olaudah describes his homeland as fertile and farming as the main activity of his people. They grew Indian corn and large crops of cotton and tobacco. Pineapples grew wild, as did a great variety of other fruits and many spices, such as pepper. Wild honey could also be found. "All our industry is exerted to improve those blessings of nature," he writes.

Everyone, including children, took part. Since everyone worked and shared with everyone else, there were no beggars. According to Olaudah, people were generally healthy, active, and vigorous. Cheerfulness and friendliness were two of the leading characteristics of Olaudah's nation.

Adults farmed on a large plain several hours' walk from where they lived, and they all went together, leaving the children behind to play. They had no animals that did farmwork, although several animals were domesticated in Africa. The people worked with hoes, axes, shovels, and pointed iron tools for digging. "Sometimes," Olaudah writes, "we are visited by locusts, which come in large clouds, so as to darken the air, and destroy our harvest. This however happens rarely, but when it does, a famine is produced by it."

A "bird of prophecy," a symbol of the king of Benin's power

Although Olaudah's people hunted wild animals for food, most of their meat came from domesticated animals, such as cattle, goats, and poultry. His people were also herders. In fact, their herds were their main source of wealth, and herd animals were among the most important items of trade. When the people used their herds for their own food, they would stew the meat in a pan, sometimes with pepper and other spices and a salt made of wood ashes. Their vegetables included plantains, yams, beans, and corn.

"The head of the family usually eats alone," writes Olaudah. "His wives and slaves have also their separate tables. Before we taste food we always wash our hands: indeed our cleanliness on all occasions is extreme; but on this it is an indispensable ceremony. After washing, libation is made, by pouring out a small portion of the food, in a certain place, for the spirits of departed relations, which the natives suppose to preside over their conduct, and guard them from evil."

Although nature provided most of his people's needs, they did make some things. They made cloth for clothing, earthenware dishes, and tools for farming and warfare. They did not have much use for money, but for trade they did have a small coin shaped something like an anchor.

They did their trading at markets, where Olaudah often went with his mother. He writes, "These are sometimes visited by stout mahogany-coloured men from the south west of us: we call them Oye-Eboe, which term signifies red men living at a distance. They generally bring us fire-arms, gunpowder, hats, beads, and dried fish. The last we esteemed a great rarity, as our waters were only brooks and springs. These articles they barter with us for odoriferous woods and earth, and our salt of wood

ashes. They always carry slaves through our land; but the strictest account is exacted of their manner of procuring them before they are suffered to pass. Sometimes indeed we sold slaves to them, but they were only prisoners of war, or such among us as had been convicted of kidnapping, or adultery, and some other crimes, which we esteemed heinous.

"I remember too," Olaudah continues, "they carried great sacks along with them, which not long after I had an opportunity of fatally seeing applied to that infamous purpose."

As noted earlier, Olaudah was eleven years old when he was kidnapped. He and his sister had been left alone to play in their yard while the adults went off to the fields. Suddenly, two men

Slave traders rounding up captured African villagers

and a woman climbed over their wall, grabbed the children, and carried them off to the nearest wood, where the captors tied the children's hands. The kidnappers then carried them for miles, keeping to the woods and stopping only at night. When at last they had to leave the woods, Olaudah saw his chance and cried out to some people he saw in the distance. His captors immediately gagged him and stuffed him into one of their large sacks. They also gagged and bound his sister.

Olaudah and his sister were finally separated, never to see each other again. He had a succession of owners and eventually was brought to the coast, where he was sold to British slavers. He was taken first to Barbados in the West Indies and then to Virginia. Eventually, he was sold to a Quaker merchant from Philadelphia who allowed him to buy his freedom in 1766.

Philadelphia in the late 1700s. It was in this "City of Brotherly Love" that Olaudah Equiano regained his freedom.

Olaudah moved to England, where he prospered. He also played an active role in the movement to abolish the slave trade. Not only did he write his autobiography and publish it himself; he also sold it by subscription—that is, people paid for it beforehand, and then he sent it to them. In addition, he toured widely in England, Scotland, and Wales. In 1792 he married an Englishwoman, Susanna Cullen. Olaudah and Susanna had two daughters, one of whom survived to inherit a substantial estate from her father.

Olaudah died in 1797, a decade before the slave trade was abolished in British shipping, forty years before slavery was outlawed in British colonies, and nearly seventy years before slavery ended in the United States. Although Olaudah did not live to see the success of abolition, his narrative was a significant factor in bringing about the end of the slave trade. In addition to the information about Africa that Olaudah relates here, his narrative tells us a great deal about his life as a slave. Many people were shocked that such an intelligent man had been enslaved.

SOME
MEMOIRS
OF THE
LIFE of JOB,
THE
SON of SOLOMON
THE
HIGH PRIEST of *Boonda*
in *Africa*;

Who was a Slave about two Years
in *Maryland*; and afterwards being
brought to *England*, was set free,
and sent to his native Land in the
Year 1734.

By THOMAS BLUETT, *Gent.*
who was intimately acquainted with him
in *America*, and came over to *England*
with him.

Chapter 3

AYUBA BEN SULEIMAN DIALLO

AYUBA BEN SULEIMAN DIALLO (1701?–AFTER 1735), our second guide to Africa, took the name Job ben Solomon as a close translation of his name in the Pular language, his native tongue. His story, told to a white resident of Maryland named Thomas Bluett, was published in London in 1734. Its full title is *Some Memoirs of the Life of Job, the Son of Solomon the High Priest of Boonda in Africa; Who Was a Slave about Two Years in Maryland; and afterwards Being Brought to England, Was Set Free, and Sent to His Native Land in the Year 1734.* The marvelous story of Ayuba's enslavement and rescue make up much of the published narrative, but other parts of it deal with customs and ways of life in his African homeland.

Ayuba had been kidnapped in 1730, when he was about thirty years old. As the title of his narrative indicates, he was

The title page of Ayuba Ben Suleiman Diallo's narrative

taken to Annapolis, Maryland, and spent two years there in slavery. Then he managed to escape from his owner, and although he was soon caught and imprisoned as a fugitive slave, he was fortunate enough to come into contact with some sympathetic people. As a Muslim who had been educated in Africa, and as the son of a high priest, or "grand imam," he seemed to be no ordinary slave. He was allowed to write to his father, and the letter found its way to a scholar in England who translated the Arabic into English and discovered Ayuba's true identity. An Englishman named James Oglethorpe, who later founded the American colony of Georgia, purchased Ayuba's freedom and took him to England. He lived for a while with an English minister and there learned about Christianity. In return, he wrote out by hand and from memory three complete copies of the Quran, the holy book of Islam. In 1735, Ayuba returned to his homeland—one of the few slaves in recorded history to do so.

This portrait of Ayuba was made in England; at his request, the artist showed him in the traditional clothes of his homeland.

Thomas Bluett describes Ayuba as about five feet ten inches tall, with long black, curly hair, pleasant-looking, but very serious. He notes that Ayuba had an extraordinary memory. Ayuba, though, did not consider his own memory anything very remarkable—he came from a land where the histories of peoples and families were not written down but memorized. He was able to write out three copies of the Quran because, as a member of a Muslim family, he had memorized the entire book by the time he was fifteen years old.

If Bluett ever admitted having forgotten something, Ayuba would laugh, saying that he himself never in his life forgot anything, and he wondered how anybody could.

As mentioned above, Ayuba was a Muslim, that is, a follower of Islam. As we hear Ayuba's story, it is helpful to know something about Islam, the major religion in his homeland. The name *Islam* comes from an Arabic word meaning "peace" or "submission." Followers of Islam practice submission to the will of God. Islam was founded by the Prophet Muhammad, who lived from around 570 to 632 on the Arabian Peninsula. Islam stressed belief in one God (in Arabic, Allah, "creator") rather than the many gods of some earlier religions. Muhammad wanted his followers to spread the faith, and many Arab traders who traveled to sub-Saharan Africa brought their religion to its people. Islam allows for great diversity, so it was possible for Africans to adopt Islam and still keep some of their traditional ways. Many of the ancient African shrines were incorporated into Muslim worship.

Arab traders and travelers carried their religion, Islam, to many parts of Africa.

Ayuba was born around 1701 in the town of Bondu in the kingdom of Futa (present-day Senegal) in west Africa. He came from a family of merchants who had long practiced Islam. About fifty years before Ayuba was born, his grandfather had founded Bondu and had been given permission by the king of Futa to be its governor and grand imam. Ayuba's grandfather handed down a decree that no one who came to Bondu for protection could be enslaved. This decree, Ayuba says, later was extended to include all people who could read and know God. As a result, many people had settled in the town, and it was large and prosperous. Bluett was under the impression that everyone in Bondu was Muslim. But European travelers to Bondu in the late eighteenth century (around 1750–1800) reported that many people there still believed in several gods (polytheism) and that Islam, as practiced by the people and by religious men, had elements of the traditional religions.

After the death of the grandfather, Ayuba's father became grand imam. As we have seen, Ayuba himself studied the Quran; and when he was fifteen years old he started assisting his father as an imam, or priest. At about the same age, he married the eleven-year-old daughter of the grand imam of Tombut. The marriage had been arranged by the two fathers. As Ayuba describes the typical marriage procedure to Bluett, the father of a young man would find a girl who he felt was suitable for his son and would visit her father to propose the match. The two fathers would then discuss the dowry the girl's father would provide for her—that is, the property she would bring to the marriage. When they had come to a decision, the two fathers and the young man would go to an imam to tell him about the agreement. That was all they had to do for the couple to be married.

But now comes the "great difficulty: how the young man shall get his wife home." Here Ayuba describes a traditional wedding custom special more to his people than to Muslims in general: "The women, cousins, and relations, take on mightily," he says, "and guard the door of the house, to prevent her being carried away; but at last the young man's presents and generosity to them, make them abate their grief. He then provides a friend, well mounted, to carry her off; but as soon as she is up on horseback, the women renew their lamentations, and rush in to dismount her. However, the man is generally successful, and rides off with his prize to the house provided for her."

Ayuba's wife gave birth to their first son two years after their marriage, when she was thirteen. Two more sons were born later. The modern versions of their names would be Abdullah, Ibrahim, and Sambal. About fifteen years later he took a second wife, the daughter of the grand imam of Tomga. She gave birth to a girl, whom they named Fatima, after a daughter of the Prophet Muhammad. Islam teaches modesty for both men and women, but especially for women, who often cover themselves in long dresses, scarves, and veils. Among Ayuba's people, a bride did not uncover her face to her husband until they had been married for three years. As a result, when Ayuba was captured he had not yet seen his second wife's face, since they had been married only about two years by then.

Ayuba says that to keep peace among his wives, a husband would divide his time equally among them. He also explains that while both men and women could leave a marriage, it was harder for a wife to do so. If a man sent his wife away, she was allowed to take her dowry and marry someone else if she chose to. If a woman left her husband, however, she had to leave her dowry with him, and she would thereafter have a bad reputation and no chance of remarrying.

Among Ayuba's people, children of both sexes were named at the age of seven days. Friends and relatives would come to the father's house for the ceremony; the father would name the child; and the imam would write the name on a piece of smooth board.

The father would then kill a cow or sheep, which was roasted and served to the guests; the leftovers were distributed to the poor. The child was then washed all over. The imam would write the child's name on a paper, which was rolled up and tied on a string around the child's neck, where it remained until it wore out or was rubbed off.

Ayuba's faith in one God was strong. Bluett reports that it was so strong that he could not understand the concept of the Christian Trinity (Father, Son, and Holy Spirit). Given a New Testament in Arabic, Ayuba read it carefully and then announced that he had found no mention of the three aspects of God in it. Bluett continues, "He showed upon all occasions a singular veneration for the name of God, and never pronounced the word Allah without a peculiar accent, and a remarkable pause: and indeed his notions of God, Providence, and a future state, were in the main very just and reasonable."

As a Muslim, Ayuba was wary of anything that seemed like idol worship. When asked to sit for his portrait, he was reluctant. After being assured that Bluett wanted the picture only to remember him by, Ayuba consented. The artist, Mr. Hoare, completed the face, then asked Ayuba what clothing he should draw. Ayuba said he would like to be drawn in the attire of his

A mosque, or Muslim house of worship, in Jenne. It is built of mud in the local style of the city.

own country. Hoare said he could not do that unless he could see such clothing or could obtain a description. Ayuba answered, "If you can't draw a dress you never saw, why do some of you painters presume to draw God, whom no one ever saw?" Ayuba's Muslim faith taught that portraits and other kinds of realistic paintings were a form of idol worship, or at least could influence people to worship a painting as some polytheists might worship an idol. Also, Muslims felt that in creating a realistic picture, the artist was trying to take on God's special role as Creator.

Ayuba recalled other customs of his people. Compared with marriages and namings, Muslim burial practices were simple. The body would be put into the ground, covered up, and prayers would be said. These prayers, he pointed out, were for the benefit of the survivors, not the dead person; Ayuba's people did not believe that prayers could help the dead person in the afterlife.

Ayuba's society in Africa was organized by class. Hunters were members of a high class; they spent most of their time pursuing elephants, not only for meat but also for the ivory tusks, which were valuable in trade. Hunters would dip their arrows in the juice of a certain tree to make a poison that would stun the animal and cause it to fall down, so that the hunter could jump onto it and cut its throat. The hunters carried an herb that served as an antidote in case they accidentally wounded themselves with a poisoned arrow.

A hunter once told Ayuba that elephants hated lions and that he had seen an elephant surprise a lion, carry it to a tree, split the tree in half, and put the lion's head through the split, leaving the lion there to die. Ayuba says that he is not sure this story is true but thinks it might be, since he himself once saw an elephant catch a lion, carry it to a large mud pit, and smother it by holding its head under the mud.

One day Ayuba found a cow of his father's dead and partly eaten. He decided to try to catch the culprits. He climbed a tree nearby and waited. That evening he saw two lions approaching the carcass with great caution, looking carefully around them, perhaps sensing danger. At last one grew brave enough, or its hunger got the better of it. It went up to the carcass. Immediately, Ayuba shot it with a poisoned arrow. Wounded, the lion roared and ran off, and the next morning Ayuba found it dead, about three hundred yards away.

Ayuba's narrative does not include much about farming. Ayuba does say, though, that slaves and the lower classes did the cultivation. He speaks of a crop which the people pulled up by the roots and rubbed between two stones to grind into flour. Bluett calls this crop "corn," but it was actually peanuts.

Ayuba's English friends apparently were dismayed to think that Africans lacked tools and machines, and when he was about to return to his homeland they gave him everything they thought could be useful to him. They took special care to explain how to use these devices. Bluett writes that Ayuba was a genius at learning the uses of machines. When shown instruments that he had never before seen, such as a clock, a gristmill, and a plow, he was able to understand how they worked and, after they were taken apart, put them back together again.

What happened to Ayuba upon his return to Africa is not certain, but we may hope that after his escape from slavery he led a long, happy life and saw to it that the European tools and machines were put to good use.

THE PEANUT

Ayuba mentions a crop that his people would pull up by the roots and grind into flour. This does indeed seem to be a very close description of peanuts, because the edible part—the part that gets eaten—grows underground, so it does need to be pulled up. The "nut" starts growing from the flower of the plant, in the open air, but then the flower stalk bends down so that the rest of the growth can take place under the soil.

The peanut is not native to Africa. It originated in South America and was brought to Africa for reasons having to do with the slave trade. Early Portuguese slavers planted it on the west African coast to provide a cheap but nourishing food for captives being held (like Broteer, whose story is told in chapter 5) until they could be boarded onto ships. By the year 1682, a missionary named Father Merolla found peanuts growing in the Congo.

In chapter 2, Olaudah mentioned locusts "which come in large clouds, so as to darken the air, and destroy our harvest." An important advantage of peanuts, once they have moved underground to ripen, is that they are better protected than most plants against locusts. Another advantage of the peanut is that it is just as nutritious as the Portuguese supposed. In Africa in modern times, it has given the highest protein yield per acre compared to other crops.

The peanut finally arrived in the United States from Africa about 1790. African-American slaves gave it the name *goober,* from a Bantu word or from the Kimbundu word *nguba*— which may actually have referred not to the peanut but to a similar plant called the Congo goober.

AN INTERESTING NARRATIVE.

BIOGRAPHY
OF
MAHOMMAH G. BAQUAQUA,

A NATIVE OF ZOOGOO, IN THE INTERIOR OF AFRICA.

(A Convert to Christianity,)

WITH A DESCRIPTION OF THAT PART OF THE WORLD:

INCLUDING THE

Manners and Customs of the Inhabitants,

Their Religious Notions. Form of Government, Laws, Appearance of the Country, Buildings, Agriculture, Manufactures, Shepherds and Herdsmen, Animals, Marriage and Funeral Ceremonies, Dress, Trade and Commerce, Warfare, Slavery, with an Account of Mahommah's early life, Education, Capture and Slavery in Africa and Brazil, Escape, Reception by Rev. W. L. Judd, Baptist Missionary at Port au Prince, Conversion to Christianity, Baptism, his Views, Objects and Aim, &c.

WRITTEN AND REVISED FROM HIS OWN WORDS,

BY SAMUEL MOORE, ESQ.,

Late publisher of the "North of England Shipping Gazette," author of several popular works, and editor of sundry reform papers.

MAHOMMAH G. BAQUAQUA,
Engraved by J. G. Darby, from a Daguerreotype by Sutton.

DETROIT:
Printed for the Author, *Mahommah Gardo Baquaqua,*
BY GEO. E. POMEROY & CO., TRIBUNE OFFICE.
1854.

Chapter 4

Mahommah Gardo Baquaqua

MAHOMMAH GARDO BAQUAQUA (1824?–AFTER 1854) is our third guide. He told his story to an American named Samuel Moore, and it was published in Detroit, Michigan, in 1854. The very long title of this book begins *An Interesting Narrative. Biography of Mahommah G. Baquaqua, a Native of Zoogoo, in the Interior of Africa. (A Convert to Christianity.) With a Description of That Part of the World; Including the Manners and Customs of the Inhabitants* . . . and goes on (and on and on) from there.

In his book Mahommah goes into detail about many aspects of life in his homeland. About how his people dressed, he describes the clothing of Muslim men and non-Muslim women. Muslim men wore loose trousers, full at the bottom and tied around the hips by a cord. Over that they wore a loose

The title page of Mahommah Gardo Baquaqua's narrative

robe, with wide sleeves and an open neck. Women wore a cloth about two yards square, doubled cornerwise and tied about the waist. Children did not wear much clothing at all.

Mahommah goes into some detail about traditional African styles of head shaving among men who were not Muslims. Men in different kingdoms shaved their heads differently, so it was possible to identify a man's region by the way he shaved his head. In Mahommah's own part of Africa, men shaved the sides of their heads and allowed the hair to grow quite long in three round spots, with the spaces between them shaved, from the forehead to the back of the head.

Mahommah was born around 1824, probably (like Olaudah) in Guinea, near a place that he calls—or that Moore wrote down as—Zoogoo. Mahommah's mother, described as a native of Kashna, was wealthy and did not, according to Mahommah, practice any religion. His father, who was a Muslim of Arab descent, had once been a successful merchant but had lost his money.

Mohammah had one brother and three sisters. Twins born before him had died in infancy. Mahommah says that Africans were very superstitious about twins, imagining that they were more knowing than other children. If a pair of twins lived, an image of them was made out of a particular wood, one for each, and the twins were taught to offer food to these "dolls" whenever they had anything to eat. If the twins died, then the next child to be born was given the twin dolls, and it would be that child's duty to feed them. Mahommah was the next born after twins in his family, and he was therefore treated specially.

Mahommah's father rose every morning at dawn for prayers. He prayed again at noon, afternoon, sunset, and evening. Once a

year, the Muslim people fasted during the month of Ramadan. They would eat nothing all day long, but after sundown and certain ceremonies, they were allowed to eat. At the end of this month-long fast, many people would assemble in a large yard that belonged to Mahommah's grandfather. Mahommah's uncle, an imam, would officiate. The people would arrange themselves in rows according to age, with the oldest people nearest to the imam. They prayed, and the imam recited passages from the Quran. They then prayed for their king, so that he would preserve the people from famine and locusts and grant them rain in due season. At the end of the ceremony, the people returned home to offer sacrifices to the dead and the living. One of the purposes of Ramadan, besides helping people feel closer to God, was to remind them what it was like to be hungry. In this way, they might be able to have more compassion for others less fortunate than themselves.

Mahommah gives more detail than Ayuba about Muslim burial practices. According to Mahommah, the body was wrapped in a white cloth and buried as soon as possible. After

Nomads in the Sahara at their evening prayers. Devout Muslims pray five times a day, no matter where they are or what they're doing.

the body was laid out, facing east (toward the Muslim holy city of Mecca in Arabia), an imam would be summoned to lead prayers to Allah for the soul of the departed. After burial, the grave was covered with a large flat stone. Mahommah says that there would be much loud mourning for six days, during which time the friends and family of the departed would shut themselves away. On the seventh day, they held a great feast to signal the end of the mourning period.

The laws by which people lived were set down in the writings of Islam. Mahommah speaks of a "law of kindness" or hospitality: "Whatever a person has, he freely divides with his neighbor, and no one even enters a house without being invited to eat."

Another custom that was practically a law concerned the treatment of old people. They were to be respected and addressed as Father or Mother (people of the same age called each other Sister or Brother). The best seats were reserved for old people, and in places of worship they always sat closest to the imam. Children were brought up to be obedient and polite and were never permitted to contradict an elderly person. They had to stand, not sit, in the presence of an old man or woman; and when they met an elder, they had to show respect by bowing.

Possibly, this Muslim tradition of respect for elders was not always observed by non-Muslims in Zoogoo who, Mahommah reports, might be superstitious and might believe in witchcraft—particularly in the possibility that they could be bewitched. A person who thought a spell had been cast on him would consult an astrologer, who would study the stars and identify the supposed witch: usually a poor old woman. She would then be put to death by medicine men called *unbahs. Unbahs* were scattered all over the country, and Mahommah tells us that the Muslims considered them very wicked people.

Mahommah's father wanted him to be a religious man and sent him to school at a mosque. This school had no books except the Quran, and no paper for writing. The students wrote on boards, which were cleaned after each lesson. Parents paid a fee for their children's schooling, but only after seeing proof that the children had mastered what they were supposed to learn. At a specific time, all the pupils and teachers would gather at a large mosque, where the parents were in attendance. Each pupil had to read twenty chapters of the Quran without missing a single word. If a student managed to do so, his education was considered finished and his school fees were paid.

Unlike his brother, who enjoyed learning Arabic and reading the Quran, Mahommah was too interested in the outside world to be a religious scholar. Since he was not a good student, he was sent to live with an uncle who was blacksmith to the king, to learn that trade. A smith was an important person, because he made the few tools that Africans used, such as knives and hoes. Mahommah's uncle also made jewelry of sil-

Medicine men played an important role in many African cultures. Sometimes they were feared, like the *unbahs* described by Mahommah, but often they were healers and religious leaders.

ver and gold—necklaces, bracelets, earrings, and finger rings. Mahommah learned how to make the jewelry as well as such tools as knives and needles. Making needles for sewing was a long and difficult process. Iron was heated and hammered into fine wire, which was cut into lengths. Then each wire was beaten and filed to a sharp point. Finally, it was polished by being rubbed on a smooth stone. Mahommah did not like such laborious work, and eventually he returned to his own household.

Mahommah gives many details about his birthplace, Zoo-goo. It was in a region of mountains and hills, forests and plains. It was fairly well watered by a white river and a nearby spring. The climate was very hot. The plains were covered with tall grasses, which the people used to thatch their houses. There were only a few trees on these plains, but those that did exist were huge. Elephants, lions, and other wild animals roamed the plains, and the tall grasses were a refuge for them.

Every so often, a message went out by way of drums that the grasses would be fired. Hunters would come from miles around and station themselves in a large circle. They would then set fires at several points around the circle so that the grasses burned inward. As animals fled the fire, the hunters shot them with bows and arrows.

Wild birds such as peacocks and guinea fowl were abundant, and the people of the forests ate their meat and their eggs. There was also an animal, Mahommah tells us, that resembled the North American beaver but was blue. It felled trees and built shelters partly above and partly in the water. People did not much bother with it, because its flesh was not good to eat and its fur was of no use for clothing. There were parrots and

singing birds in the forests; and in the rivers there were crocodiles and huge turtles, whose shells were used as small boats.

The soil was so rich that a single acre could yield a huge crop. Mahommah's people used large hoes to dig up the ground and small hoes to plant the crops. They raised rice in great quantities, since it would come up again by itself for two or three years without being replanted. Other crops included sweet potatoes and corn.

Women ground the corn. They put the dried kernels on a large stone on the earth, then took a smaller stone that was grooved on one side and rubbed this over the corn until it was ground fine. Another method of grinding was to use a hollowed-out log as a huge mortar. To make this device, a group of men would go into the forest, select an enormous tree of a particular kind, cut it down, and cut off a log about four feet long. Mahommah did not say what kind of tree was used, but the African baobab tree, for example, can be thirty feet

This scene, painted by a British artist-explorer in 1805, shows some of the rich plant and animal life of tropical Africa.

wide. The men would hollow this gigantic log out and make the inside smooth. When it was ready, the king would invite a large number of men to roll it to his house and place it where he directed. The mortar was so wide in circumference that ten or fifteen people could work at it together, using smaller logs as pestles, to grind up corn, yams, and other vegetables.

People mixed ground yams with a grain called *harnee* to make a stiff pudding, which they served with a sauce made of greens and various other vegetables and seasoned with pepper and onions. No food, Mahommah adds, was ever eaten without onions.

Cotton grew abundantly, and most of the people's clothing was made of it. Women twisted the fibers into thread. Men then wove the threads into narrow strips of cloth, which were sewn together.

Mahommah describes Zoogoo itself as a large city surrounded by a thick wall of red clay that was smoothed and polished. Outside the wall was a deep moat or ditch, which filled with water during the rainy season. "The entrance into the city is through six gates," the narrative continues, "which bear the names of their respective keepers, something similar to the city of London and most of the old fortified towns in England." The king also appointed watchmen to make regular patrols.

The king's compound was inside the city wall, surrounded by grass and trees and protected at the back by a dense thicket. It was set apart from the center of the city, and a broad avenue led from the city to it. On either side of the king's house were market stalls, shaded by large overhanging trees.

Trade with outsiders centered on salt, which was brought in on horses and donkeys from a place Mahommah calls Sab-ba

CORN

Were you surprised to read Mahommah's description of grinding corn? Many people associate corn, or maize, mainly with the Americas, where it originated. But corn was also known, and grown, in Africa—and like the peanut, it had links to the slave trade.

For one thing, some traders used American corn to buy slaves from Africa. Dried corn kept well on the long ocean voyage to Africa, and it was in demand there. The slaves who were sold for corn might then be taken to America by ship in the same holds that had carried the corn; and on arrival they might work on corn plantations, whose produce then went to buy more slaves. As early as 1535, a traveler named John Leo met a tribe on the Niger River who had stored up large amounts of corn, and in the twentieth century Africans in Zambia and other places where maize is grown still stored dried corn kernels in underground pits.

In North America, corn was (and is) often used as fodder for livestock, but in Africa only cornstalks or hulls removed from the kernels would be fed to cattle—the kernel itself was prized highly and was for humans to eat. The Yoruba people (in what is now Nigeria) made corn into a mush called *ogi*, a process that took several days and involved soaking, grinding, and boiling. *Agidi* is a corn mush wrapped in banana leaves and then cooked, in Sierra Leone and Ivory Coast; a similar dish in Ghana is called *kenkey*. Corn might be mixed with other foods, such as red peppers and peanuts—and onions, if Mahommah is not exaggerating when he says that onions were eaten with everything. Africans might also dip corn in relish, possibly the origin of Americans' fondness for chips and dips.

and was exchanged for ivory, cows, and slaves. Occasionally European goods were brought in from Ashantee (the Ashanti kingdom), but they were very expensive.

The typical household was made of up members of an extended family. They lived in a number of separate one-room buildings made of clay. Each family unit had its own dwelling. The houses were arranged in a circle and enclosed by a wall. A large household would have a second circle of buildings surrounding the inner circle. There was one large main entrance for receiving company, but otherwise the household compound was very private. Because these compounds took up a good deal of space, cities were spread over a wide area.

Like Ayuba, Mahommah saw different customs and climates after he was kidnapped, then sold and resold as he was marched toward the coast. In a city called Dohama he and his owner encountered a woman. His owner immediately ran away and commanded Mahommah to follow him. Mahommah learned that the woman was the king's wife and that it was a mark of respect for her subjects to run away when they saw her. The people in another place, called Cham-mah, were hunters who went around "nearly naked and are of the rudest description."

Mahommah saw some beautiful scenery: "The country through which we passed after leaving Chir-a-chir-ee was quite hilly, water abundant and of good quality, the trees are very large; we did not suffer anything from heat on the journey, as the weather was quite cool and pleasant . . .; the flowers are various and beautiful, the trees, full of birds, large and small, some sing very delightfully. We crossed several large streams of water, which had it not been the dry season, would have been very deep, as it was they were easily forded, being no more than three feet of water in some places. There were great quantities of aquatic birds sporting about; we saw [some that looked like] swans in abundance, we tried to kill some, but found it very difficult, as their movements are very quick upon the water; they have a most beautiful appearance when on the wing, the necks and wings extended in the air, they are perfectly white, never fly very high nor far away; their flesh is sweet and good, and considered a great dish."

African captives were often chained together with forked sticks during their journey to the slave markets.

Mahommah was to see much more. His journey as a slave took him to South America, where he was bought by a ship's captain with whom he traveled widely. While his ship was docked at the port of New York, his cause was taken up by some members of the antislavery movement. Those abolitionists first urged the captain to free Mahommah. When the captain would not do so, they helped Mahommah escape. They then sent him to Boston and from there to Haiti. In Haiti, he lived with a Baptist missionary who taught him the Christian faith. Mahommah proved to be an eager student and was later sent to upstate New York for further study. After that, the plan was for Mahommah to return to his homeland to convert his people to Christianity. Whether he ever did so is not known. But he did visit Canada, where he felt especially welcome. Eventually, he moved to Canada and became a subject of the British Empire.

This diagram of a
slave ship shows how
the captives were
crammed together
belowdecks for the
voyage across the
Atlantic.

Chapter 5

BROTEER, CALLED VENTURE SMITH

OUR FOURTH GUIDE IS BROTEER (1729?–1805). IN AMERICA, he went by the name of Venture Smith. Venture was a name given to him by his first owner, and he took the name Smith after a later owner, who allowed him to buy his freedom. His life story, told to an American editor, was published in New London, Connecticut, in 1798.

No picture of Broteer survives, but we do have a description. He was a huge man, straight and tall, weighing more than three hundred pounds and measuring six feet around the waist. "I descended from a very large, tall and stout race of being, much larger than the generality of people in other parts of the globe," he explains. He must have seemed an extraordinary being indeed to the people he met in his travels.

Like Olaudah and, possibly, Mahommah, Broteer was born

in the region called Guinea on the west coast of Africa. His descriptions of his travels suggest that his homeland was probably the northern part of this region, far from the seacoast and close to the great Sahara.

When Broteer was six, he tells us, his family was set upon by a large army of Africans "instigated by some white nation," who killed his father and forced the rest into slavery. After a long march to the seacoast, during which there were several battles, he was sold to the captain of a slave ship. He was then bought by the ship's steward, and next he was sold in Rhode Island. He then had several owners, but eventually he managed to buy his freedom with money he had earned by hiring out his labor. He then bought his wife and sons. In his later years, he owned slaves himself, as well as a hundred-acre farm and three houses. He died in East Haddam, Connecticut, in 1805.

Because he was so young when he was kidnapped, Broteer had fewer memories of African life than our other three guides. However, he did spend several months in Africa after the kidnapping and was witness to not only battles but also the ways in which villagers tried to protect themselves.

Broteer's father, Saungm Furro, king of the Dukandarra people, had three wives. Broteer was the

Broteer's tombstone, in a churchyard in East Haddam, Connecticut, memorializes the hard work that enabled him to earn the money to buy his freedom.

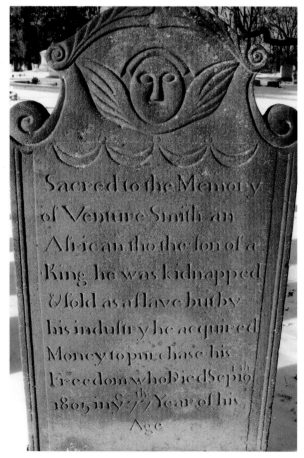

eldest of three children by the first wife. There were two children by the second wife, and one child by the third. They were all big people.

One of Broteer's first memories was a dispute between his father and his mother. His father had failed to follow custom and had taken a third wife without asking the consent of the first, Broteer's mother. She took her children and set off to the east, bound for her own homeland. Broteer was then five years old.

He was old enough to walk, but his mother carried the other two children on her back. Perhaps that is why she took no food or other provisions. They walked endlessly, Broteer recalls, stopping every now and then to rest. Fruits were plentiful in the land they were traveling through, and his mother would gather them for food. The first night, they lay together at the base of a large tree. Although they could hear the cries of wild animals, none threatened them.

Broteer remembers that on the second day they arrived at a great desert, and that while traveling through it he heard the howling of wolves, lions, and other animals. But again they were not attacked. After five days of desert travel, they arrived in a beautiful countryside. There, the mother left Broteer with a rich farmer she knew, while she continued on to her native village with the two younger children.

Broteer estimates that they had traveled about 140 miles from his home to this country beyond the desert. A large river ran through the land. On either side of it, for a great distance, the countryside was flat. Although there was little rain, the land was fertile, for the river caused dew to form at night, and the dew watered the soil. Around the end of June or the first of

July, the river would begin to rise and would continue rising until it had flooded the entire country around to a depth of seven or eight feet. When the waters subsided, they left a layer of silt that greatly enriched the soil.

Most of the people farmed and herded. They were not as large as the people in Broteer's homeland. The farmer, Broteer's guardian, had a huge flock of sheep, and Broteer helped tend the flock. The farmer also had herds of cattle and goats.

After many months, a man arrived on horseback. He had been sent by Broteer's father to claim the little boy, and to pay the farmer for keeping him. When Broteer arrived home, he was delighted to find his mother and the two younger children. His parents had patched up their differences, and the family was reunited.

Barely six weeks later, a messenger arrived from the place where Broteer had stayed for nearly a year. That place, Broteer says, "had been invaded by a numerous army, from a nation not far distant, furnished with musical instruments, and all kinds of arms then in use; . . . they were instigated by some white nation who equipped and sent them to subdue and possess the country." The messenger asked if Broteer's father would give the people refuge in his kingdom, and the king agreed.

The refugees had not been in Broteer's kingdom longer than four days when word came that the enemy army had followed them. Soon, a messenger from the army arrived to demand a large sum of money, as well as three hundred fat cattle and a great number of goats, sheep, and other livestock. To protect his people, the king agreed to those terms. But soon he received a warning that the enemy had no intention of keeping their part of the bargain and were preparing to attack.

The king, his three wives and six children, and other members of the household hurriedly packed up and made for a large shrub plain, where they thought they could hide safely. But the enemy army saw their cooking fire and attacked. While the women and children hid in the reeds, the king stood his ground. He could not fight alone, however, and was forced to surrender. Demanding to know where his money was hidden, the attackers tortured him until he died, while his family watched helplessly. Broteer tells us, "The shocking scene is to this day fresh in my mind, and I have often been overcome [with grief] while thinking on it."

The attackers then seized the women and children, tied their hands, bound them together with ropes around their necks, and set off westward toward the coast, where they knew that they

Roped-together captives are marched away from their village. This pictorial record was made by a European artist in 1795.

would find eager buyers for the captives. The enemy army was huge, numbering about six thousand. Its leader was called Baukurre. "The enemy had remarkable success in destroying the country wherever they went," Broteer reports. "For as far as they had penetrated, they laid the habitations waste and captured the people."

In a place called Malagasco, the inhabitants put up a strong fight. Broteer remembers that when Baukurre's army arrived, no houses or people could be seen. But a search revealed that instead of freestanding homes, the people had made caves inside small hills near ponds and streams of water. These caves were about eight feet deep, six feet high, and six feet wide.

Baukurre decided to smoke the people out by putting burning sticks at the entrances to the caves. Suddenly, the attackers were surprised by a rain of arrows, which came from holes at the tops of the caves. The tips of the arrows had been dipped in poison, but Baukurre's army had an antidote, which they instantly rubbed on their wounds. In spite of their courageous and clever defense, the villagers could not remain in their smoky caves. They came out and were immediately tied up. Their herds and possessions were taken as well.

Baukurre's army then continued marching toward the sea. But they were burdened with many people and animals, their provisions were low, and they were weakened from so much fighting. At a place called Anamaboo, which Broteer calculates was about four hundred miles from his home, the people were ready for them. Instead of waiting for Baukurre to attack, they struck first, capturing all the prisoners, herds, and other possessions. "I was then taken a second time," Bro-

Guarded by a spearman, captives imprisoned in a shed wait to be sent on the next stage of their journey into slavery.

teer says. "All of us were then put into the castle [a European slave-trading post] and kept for market."

As we have seen, after being bought by the steward of the slave ship, Broteer was sold in Rhode Island. Before he was finally able to buy his freedom, he had married a slave woman and they had had sons. Eventually, he earned enough money to purchase his freedom as well as that of his wife and sons. When he died, in 1805, emancipation was still about sixty years in the future.

A noble warrior from Benin in the sixteenth or seventeenth century. He wears a necklace of leopard teeth to show that he fights as fiercely as a leopard.

Chapter 6

Warfare and Slavery in Africa

THE NARRATIVES OF OUR GUIDES TELL US NOT ONLY about daily life in Africa but also about warfare and slavery there. For instance, Broteer's experience as the prisoner of a large marauding army makes it clear how important the transatlantic slave trade had become in the part of Africa called Guinea. By the 1750s, that trade was the main cause of war in the region—a significant change from earlier times.

Warfare had long been common in Africa. Mahommah explains that, like Europe, Africa was comprised of many kingdoms, and the kings were continually quarreling. Also, when a king died, it was not always clear who should be the new king, and sometimes arguments over succession led to warfare. According to Mahommah, "When a king dies, there is no regular successor, but a great many rivals for the kingdom spring up, and he who can achieve his object by power and strength, becomes the succeeding king; thus war settles the question." Furthermore, war was a way to gain more land or consolidate power. And when one region suffered a famine, its people might go great distances to steal food and livestock from others.

Olaudah writes that the people of Iboland were always prepared for war: "We have fire-arms, bows and arrows, broad two-edged swords and javelins: we have shields also which cover a man from head to foot. All are taught the use of these weapons; even our women are warriors, and march boldly out to fight along with the men. Our whole district is a kind of militia: on a certain signal given, such as the firing of a gun at night, they all rise in arms and rush upon their enemy." He reports that when the people expected an attack, they made a fence around their houses by driving sharp-pointed sticks dipped in poison into the ground.

Olaudah also writes that when the people of his village went out to till their land, they went as a group and took their arms with them. He was once with his people when they were attacked. Taking cover in a tree, he witnessed the battle: "There were many women as well as men on both sides; among others my mother was there, and armed with a broad sword. After fighting for a considerable time with great fury, and after many had been killed, our people obtained the victory, and took their enemy's chief prisoner. He was carried off in great triumph, and, though he offered a large ransom for his life, he was put to death. . . . The spoils were divided according to the merit of the warriors. Those prisoners which were not sold or redeemed we kept as slaves."

AFRICA: A LOOK BACK

Slaves had been among the spoils of war for centuries, and slavery in Africa—as in other parts of the world—went back to ancient times. However, a strong tradition had developed that governed the place of slaves in African societies and guaranteed them certain rights and responsibilities.

Olaudah writes of slaves, "With us they do no more work than other members of the community, even their masters; their food, clothing and lodging were nearly the same as theirs (except that they were not permitted to eat with those who were free-born); and there was scarce any other difference between them. . . . Some of these slaves have even slaves under them as their own property, and for their own use."

WHY DOES WAR EXIST?

There have been various theories of why humans make war on each other. One popular idea, which has persisted for a long time, is that humans are hardwired for war, that the urge to fight is an instinct. This idea is based on the fact that almost every culture on Earth, throughout history, has waged war. But another theory is that war is not instinctive—it is, instead, a way for people to take what they want, and particularly to steal what they want. The scientist Jacob Bronowski, for instance, said that war is a highly planned, cooperative form of theft which originated 10,000 years ago when nomads—who could accumulate little—swooped down on settled communities to take stored food.

Warfare intended to capture slaves is, perhaps, strong evidence for the "theft" theory, because Africans who were kidnapped, like our four narrators, were in fact being stolen from their homes and families for just one purpose: to be sold and earn a profit for the sellers.

What other reasons can you think of that make people go to war?

A slave trade with Arabs in the north had been conducted for centuries. There, too, slaves had rights as well as responsibilities. The Quran dealt in some detail with slaves, who were to be regarded as people, not simply as possessions.

Slavery in Africa and on the Arabian Peninsula was thus very different from slavery in the European colonies in the New World. The type of slavery practiced in the New World was chattel slavery, in which slaves were not regarded as people. These slaves had no more rights than livestock or other personal property. Chattel slavery was a brutal system, and it involved many slaves. The need for labor in the New World was so great that during the height of the slave trade, between 1750 and 1800, many millions of slaves were taken out of Africa. This was the approximate period when our four narrators were captured and enslaved.

The transatlantic slave trade changed African society. In the early days, when the Portuguese and then the Dutch and others began to export slaves from Africa, it was a trade like any other. African kings controlled the trade on their end and were eager to exchange their own slaves for goods from Europe. Affonso I, ruler of the Kingdom of Kongo, on the western coast below the equator, oversaw the slave trade in his domain from 1525 to 1540. But as early as 1526, he wrote to King João III of Portugal to complain that the trade was out of control. He explained that his people were so intent on obtaining Portuguese goods that they were kidnapping "freed and exempt men . . . even noblemen and the sons of noblemen, and our relatives." Affonso protested that his country was becoming "completely depopulated."

But not even a king could stop the transatlantic trade in

A wealthy African slave trader in his luxuriously furnished bedroom

African slaves. As time went on, the coastal areas were indeed depopulated, and slavers had to go farther into the interior. Slave ships sailed on the great rivers into the continent, where they anchored and exchanged goods for slaves provided by local traders. Enterprising slave traders went hundreds and even thousands of miles inland from the coastal areas, and marauding bands of slave catchers roamed the countryside, capturing whole villages.

Olaudah writes that he believed more African slaves were procured by kidnapping than in any other way. He himself had been kidnapped, as were our other three guides.

All of Africa suffered as a result of the slave trade. African economies, which had once been based on enhancing and conserving natural resources, were completely disrupted. So many European goods arrived in payment for slaves, gold, ivory, spices, and other natural resources that many African crafts-people, including textile workers and metalworkers, stopped making their special products. Most tragically, millions of the youngest, strongest, and healthiest people were forced from their homeland and compelled to use their skills, strength, and intelligence in a strange new world.

Glossary

abolish To do away with; to bring to an end. The people who worked to end slavery were called abolitionists.

afterlife Continued existence following death. Different cultures and religions have different ideas about an afterlife.

antidote Medicine to prevent or cure the effects of poisoning.

astrologer Someone who attempts to predict human traits and events according to the apparent positions of the stars and planets in the sky. The word for this practice is *astrology*. (Astrology has no basis in fact. Do not confuse it with astronomy, which is a real science—the study of everything in space beyond the earth's atmosphere.)

chattel slavery A system in which slaves are considered property, like livestock, tools, or furniture.

colonize To send out people—colonists—from one nation to live in and govern another. Often, one nation colonizes another by first conquering it.

depopulate To cause a sharp decrease in the population (number of inhabitants) of an area. A depopulated region has lost a significant percentage of its people.

ethnic group People linked by race, nationality, language, tribal membership, or culture.

fugitive Runaway.

idealize To look only at the good side of something, such as a place or person.

infamous Evil; wicked.

javelin A light spear.

libation An offering of food or liquid, often poured onto the ground, to a god or spirit.

mortar A container in which grains or spices are ground to a powder.

mosque In Islam, a place of worship.

Muslims Followers of Islam, the religion founded by the Prophet Muhammad.

narrative A story; an account of events. The person who tells the story is the narrator.

nomadic Moving from place to place rather than living in a permanent settlement. People whose way of life is nomadic are called nomads.

pestle A grinding tool, used with a mortar.

polytheism Belief in several gods. (Belief in only one god is called monotheism.)

Quran The holy book of Islam.

Ramadan In Islam, a month of fasting (going without food) from sunup to sundown.

serfs Rural people bound to the land—that is, bound to work for a landowner. Serfs were not slaves, but they were not free either.

sub-Saharan South of the Sahara.

transatlantic Spanning or crossing the Atlantic Ocean.

To Find Out More

BOOKS

Boyd, Herbert. *African History for Beginners.* Part I, *African Dawn—A Diasporan View.* New York: Writers and Readers, 1991.

Haskins, James, and Kathleen Benson. *African Beginnings.* New York: Lothrop, Lee, and Shepard, 1998.

Haskins, Jim, and Joann Biondi. *From Afar to Zulu: A Dictionary of African Cultures.* New York: Walker, 1995.

McKissack, Patricia C., and Fredrick L. McKissack. *The Royal Kingdoms of Ghana, Mali, and Songhay: Life in Medieval Africa*. New York: Holt, 1995.

Millar, Heather. *The Kingdom of Benin in West Africa*. New York: Benchmark Books, 1997.

Musgrove, Margaret. *Ashanti to Zulu: African Traditions*. New York: Puffin, 1992.

Service, Pamela F. *The Ancient African Kingdom of Kush*. New York: Benchmark Books, 1998.

WEB SITES*

Africans in America: The Terrible Transformation. WGBH Interactive and PBS Online. Copyright © 1998, 1999 WGBH Educational Foundation
http://www.pbs.org/wgbh/aia/part1/title.html

African Timelines: African Slave Trade and European Imperialism. © 1997–2005 Cora Agatucci, Professor of English, Humanities Department, Central Oregon Community College.
http://web.cocc.edu/cagatucci/classes/hum211/timelines/htimeline3.htm

Documenting the American South: North American Slave Narratives. © 2004 University Library, University of North Carolina at Chapel Hill.
http://docsouth.unc.edu/neh/texts.html

Olaudah Equiano: The Interesting Narrative of the Life of Olaudah Equiano, or Gustavus Vassa, the African. Hanover Historical Texts Project. © 1998–2005 Hanover College.
http://history.hanover.edu/texts/equiano/equiano_contents.html

The Story of Africa: Slavery. BBC World Service. © BBC 2005.
http://www.bbc.co.uk/worldservice/africa/features/storyofafrica/index_section9.shtml

Understanding Slavery: A Slave on Three Continents. Discovery School. © 2005 Discovery.com.
http://school.discovery.com/schooladventures/slavery/equiano.html

*Web site addresses sometimes change. The addresses here were all available when this book was sent to press. For more online sources, check with the media specialist at your local library.

Bibliography

Adams, Laurie Schneider. *Art across Time.* New York: McGraw-Hill, 1999.

Angier, Natalie. "Is War Our Biological Destiny?" In *The New York Times Guide to Essential Knowledge: A Desk Reference for the Curious Mind.* New York: St. Martin's, 2004.

Bluett, Thomas. *Some Memoirs of the Life of Job, the Son of Solomon the High Priest of Boonda in Africa. . . .* London: R. Ford, 1734.

Bronowski, J. *The Ascent of Man.* Boston, MA: Little, Brown, 1973.

Davidson, Basil. *African Civilization Revisited: From Antiquity to Modern Times.* Trenton, NJ: Africa World, 1993.

Equiano, Olaudah. *The Interesting Narrative of the Life of Olaudah Equiano, or Gustavus Vassa, the African. . . .* 2 vols. London: privately printed, 1789. (This was considered a true account until recent years, when some historians started to raise questions. Olaudah, they believe, was not born in Africa, had never visited Africa, and relied on the recollections of other slaves or his own reading for the early part of his narrative—though not to deceive the public. Rather, they think, he included the real experiences of many slaves so as to make the strongest possible argument against slavery and the slave trade. However, these critics have not proved their case, and many other historians tend to accept the narrative.)

Kamien, Roger. *Music: An Appreciation.* 6th ed. New York: McGraw-Hill, 1996.

Kaplan, Sidney. *The Black Presence in the Era of the American Revolution, 1770–1800.* New York: New York Graphic Society, with Smithsonian Institution Press, 1978.

Moore, Samuel, ed. *An Interesting Narrative. Biography of Mahommah G. Baquaqua, a Native of Zoogoo. . . .* Detroit, MI: George E. Pomeroy, 1854. (Although Moore's renditions of African names are hard to verify, Mahommah's existence and some of the later parts of his story have been confirmed in other writings.)

Root, Waverly. *Food.* New York: Simon and Schuster, 1980.

Smith, Venture. *A Narrative of the Life and Adventures of Venture, a Native of Africa. . . .* New London, CT: C. Holt at The Bee-Office, 1798.

University of North Carolina at Chapel Hill Libraries. *Documenting the*

American South: North American Slave Narratives, Beginnings to 1920. http://docsouth.unc.edu/neh/neh.html

Visser, Margaret. *Much Depends on Dinner.* New York: Grove, 1986.

Index

Page numbers for illustrations are in boldface.

laws, Muslim, 40

Mahommah Gardo Baquaqua, **36**, 37–44, 46–47, 57–58
marriage, 16–17, 30–31
medicine men, 41, **41**
Moore, Samuel, 37, 38
Muhammad, Prophet, 29
music and celebrations, 17, 18, **18**, **19**
Muslim culture, 4, 28–33, **32**, 37–41, **39**

Nile River, 1, 2
nomads, 8, **8**, **39**

Oglethorpe, James, 28
Olaudah Equiano, **12**, 13–25, 58, 59, 61

peanuts, 34, 35
Philadelphia, 24, **24**
politics, 9

religion, 17, 19–20
    Christianity, 9, 11, 28, 32, 47
    Islamic and Muslim practices, 28, 29, 30, 31, 32, 38–39
    mosque, **32**, 41

Sahara Desert, 2, 8, **39**
serfs, 10
slavery
    abolition of, 25, 47
    in Africa and Europe, 10, 14, **47**, **53**, **55**
    Arab slave trade, 60

Ayuba's enslavement, 27–28, 31
Broteer's enslavement, 50, 53–55, 57
chattel, 60
Mahommah's enslavement, 46–47
Olaudah's enslavement, 15, 23–24, 61
slave ships, **48**, 61
slave traders, **23**, 61, **61**
slaves as spoils of war, 59
transatlantic slave trade, **6**, 9, 11, 57, 60–61
Songhai empire, 4–5, 11

Timbuktu, city of, 2, 4, 5, **5**
trade, 1, 2, 4, 5, **10**, 11, 22–23, 29, **29**, 44, 46

warfare, 7–8, 10, 52–54, **56**, 57–58, 59
witchcraft, 40–41

About the Authors

JAMES HASKINS was Professor of English at the University of Florida and lived in Gainesville, FL, and New York City. Author of more than 100 books for adults, young adults, and children, he received awards for his work in all three areas, including the John and Patricia Beatty Award of the California Library Association (2004); the *Washington Post* Children's Book Guild Award for his body of work in nonfiction for young people (1994); the Alabama Library Association Award for best work for children (1988); the ASCAP Deems Taylor Award for excellence in writing in the field of music (1979); and numerous Coretta Scott King and Carter G. Woodson awards.

KATHLEEN BENSON is Curator of Community Projects at the Museum of the City of New York. She coedited the volume of essays *A Community of Many Worlds: Arab Americans in New York City* (2002) in connection with a major exhibition of the same title, and has coauthored several books with Jim Haskins, with whom she shared the ASCAP Deems Taylor Award for excellence in writing in the field of music in 1979.

DATE DUE

JUN 2 0			

GAYLORD · · PRINTED IN U.S.A.